TRANSFORMATION THROUGH BROKENNESS

Monet's Garden Painting Series

MARY SORRELLS

WestBow Press books may be ordered through booksellers or by contacting:

WestBow Press
A Division of Thomas Nelson & Zondervan
1663 Liberty Drive
Bloomington, IN 47403
www.westbowpress.com
1 (866) 928-1240

Because of the dynamic nature of the Internet, any web addresses or links contained in this book may have changed since publication and may no longer be valid. The views expressed in this work are solely those of the author and do not necessarily reflect the views of the publisher, and the publisher hereby disclaims any responsibility for them.

Any people depicted in stock imagery provided by Thinkstock are models, and such images are being used for illustrative purposes only.
Certain stock imagery © Thinkstock.

Scripture taken from the New King James Version. Copyright © 1979, 1980, 1982 by Thomas Nelson, Inc. Used by permission. All rights reserved.

Scripture taken from the King James Version of the Bible.

Scripture taken from the Holy Bible, NEW INTERNATIONAL VERSION®. Copyright © 1973, 1978, 1984 by Biblica, Inc. All rights reserved worldwide. Used by permission. NEW INTERNATIONAL VERSION® and NIV® are registered trademarks of Biblica, Inc. Use of either trademark for the offering of goods or services requires the prior written consent of Biblica US, Inc.
Serenity Prayer" (www.whatchristianswanttoknow.com)

ISBN: 978-1-5127-2460-8 (sc)
ISBN: 978-1-5127-2461-5 (e)

Library of Congress Control Number: 2015921198

Print information available on the last page.
WestBow Press rev. date: 01/07/2016

WESTBOW
PRESS®
A DIVISION OF THOMAS NELSON
& ZONDERVAN

Dedication

This book is dedicated to my family, friends, and students who continue to inspire me every day. And most of all, to God, the ultimate source of all creation.

Acknowledgments

I great fully acknowledge the many people throughout my life who have contributed to my art-filled journey including:

* To professional artist, Pat Fiorello for her invaluable art instruction and igniting my passion for painting while in Monet's Garden, Giverny, France.

* To Rich and Caroline Nuckolls of "Art Colony Giverny" for making this opportunity possible.

* To my dear friend Mary Hilger for inviting me to join her on the adventure of a lifetime studying in France.

* To my spiritual community for giving me strength and support during the "ups and downs" of my life.

* To God for the many blessings which He bestows on me each and every day.

Introduction

Life presents many opportunities, and I have been fortunate enough to grow as an artist and paint in Monet's Garden in Giverny, France. This high point as an artist was like juxtapose in conjunction with one of the most challenging times in my life.

The creation of each of the paintings in this book was part of a healing process which enabled me to move forward in the face of these difficulties. My intent in sharing my personal journey is to uplift and provide hope for whatever you may encounter in your own life.

As I created each painting, I listened to my intuition to guide and reveal scriptural titles and Biblical verses which captured the spirit of that creative experience. My prayer and hope is that you will find peace, comfort and healing as you reflect on each of the pages in this book.

Serenity

God grant me the serenity
To accept the things I cannot change;
Courage to change the things I can;
and wisdom to know the difference.

Living one day at a time;
Enjoying one moment at a time;
Accepting hardships as the pathway to peace;
Taking, as He did, this sinful world
As it is, not as I would have it;
Trusting that He will make all things right
If I surrender to His Will;
That I may be reasonably happy in this life
and supremely happy with Him
Forever in the next.
Amen

Standing Alone

Psalm 147:3 "He heals the brokenhearted and binds up their wounds."

Strength and Courage

Psalm 27:14 "Wait on the Lord, be of good courage, and he shall strengthen thine heart: wait, I say, on the Lord."

Outer Beauty

Psalm 139:14 "I will praise thee; for I am fearfully and wonderfully made: marvellous are thy works; and that my soul knoweth right well."

Poppy Fields of Giverny

Psalm 96:12 "Let the field be joyful, and all that is therin: then shall all the trees of the wood rejoice"

Blossoming with Color

Galations 5:22 "But the fruit of the Spirit is love, joy, peace, long suffering, kindness, goodness, faithfulness,"

Bridging the Gap

Mark 10:9 "What therefore God has joined together, let not man not separate."

Tangled in Color

Psalm 23:1-3 "The Lord is my shepherd; I shall not want. He maketh me to lie down in green pastures; he leadeth me beside the still waters. He restoreth my soul: he leadeth me in the paths of righteousness for his name's sake."

Gloomy Days Ahead

2 Chronicles 20:15 "And he said, Hearken ye, all Judah, and ye inhabitants of Jerusalem, and thou king Jehoshaphat, Thus saith the Lord unto you, Be not afraid nor dismayed by reason of this great multitude; for the battle is not yours but God's."

Lifelong Passion

Psalm 100:4 "Enter into his gates with thanksgiving, and into his courts with praise: be thankful unto him, and bless his name.

Contrasting Colors Made Complementary

Psalm 45:7 "Thou lovest righteousness, and hatest wickedness: therefore God, thy God, hath anointed thee with the oil of gladness above thy fellows."

At Peace With God

Romans 15:13 "Now the God of hope fill you with all joy and peace as you trust in him, so that you may overflow with hope by the power of the Holy Spirit."

Seeking the Light

Proverbs 3:5-6 "Trust in the Lord with all your heart and lean not on your own understanding; in all your ways acknowledge him, and he will make your paths straight."

Doors to Glory

Matthew 7:7 "Ask and it will be given to you; seek and you will find; knock and the door will be opened to you."

Gazing Ahead

John 14:13 "And whatsoever ye shall ask in my name, that will I do, that the Father may be glorified in the Son."

Faith, Hope and Love

1 Corinthians 13:13 "And now these three remain: faith, hope and love. But the greatest of these is love."

Building Trust

1 John 4:18 "There is no fear in love, but perfect love casteth out fear: because fear hath torment. He that feareth is not made perfect in love."

Growing in the Spirit

Ephesians 4:15 "But speaking the truth in love, may grow up into him in all things, which is the head, even Christ."

Field of Hopes and Dreams

Jeremiah 29:11 "For I know the plans I have for you, declares the Lord, plans to prosper you and not to harm you, plans to give you hope and a future."

Breakthrough

Romans 5:1 "Therefore being justified by faith, we have peace with God through our Lord Jesus Christ:"

Reflections of a Lifetime

Romans 8:28 "And we know that in all things God works for the good of those who love him, who have been called according to his purpose."

Moments of Memories and Joy

John 15:11 "These things I have spoken unto you, that my joy might remain in you, and that your joy might be full."

Field of Inner Growth

2 Corinthians 4:16 "Therefore we do not lose heart, but though our outer man is decaying, yet our inner man is being renewed day by day."

Peace and Tranquility

John 14:27 "Peace I leave with you, my peace I give unto you: not as the world giveth, give I unto you. Let not your heart be troubled, neither let it be afraid."

Let it Go...And Let God

Psalm 37: 3-6 "Trust in the Lord and do good...Delight thyself also in the Lord: and he shall give thee the desires of thine heart."

New Hope

Romans 5:2-5 "Through him we have also obtained access by faith into this grace in which we stand, and we rejoice in hope of the Glory of God. More than that, we rejoice in our sufferings, knowing that suffering produces endurance, and endurance produces character, and character produces hope, and hope does not put us to shame, because God's love has been poured into our hearts through the Holy Spirit who has been given to us."

About the Author

Mary Sorrells has had a passion for art all of her life. She is a professional artist and art educator who paints from the heart in an impressionistic style. Mary has taught and inspired children to paint for over twenty-five years. She has been recognized with national and state grants, including the Lilly Teacher Creativity Fellowship Award. In 2012, Mary was named Outstanding Elementary Art Educator of the Year for the state of Indiana. She earned BA and MA degrees from Ball State University and has completed professional development in Italy, Mexico, and France. Mary's fine art has received recognition including third place in The Feta de la Peinture in Giverny, France, followed by an exhibit there. She currently resides in Brookville, Indiana.

Printed in the United States
By Bookmasters